POEMS OF LOVE AND LONGING

poems of ♥ love and longing

Edited by Viv Sayer

Pont

Published in 2008 by Pont Books, an imprint of
Gomer Press, Llandysul, Ceredigion, SA44 4JL
www.gomer.co.uk

ISBN 978 1 84323 815 7
A CIP record for this title is available from the British Library.

Copyright © individual poems: the contributors, 2008
Copyright © the collection: Gomer Press, 2008

The authors assert their moral rights under the Copyright, Designs and Patents
Act, 1988 to be identified as authors of their respective works.

All rights reserved. No part of this book may be reproduced, stored in a
retrieval system, or transmitted in any form or by any means, electronic,
electrostatic, magnetic tape, mechanical, photocopying, recording or otherwise
without permission in writing from the above publishers.

This book is published with the financial support of the Welsh Books Council.

Printed and bound in Wales at Gomer Press, Llandysul, Ceredigion

Contents

Preface		vii
Room	Gillian Clarke	1
Hardly a Haiku	Julie Rainsbury	6
Show	Owen Sheers	12
Houndlove	Chris Kinsey	17
Love	Rex Harley	26
In love (NOT)	Gwyneth Glyn	32
Rejection	Jenny Sullivan	38
Angharad's First Spring	Christine Evans	46
True North	Susan Richardson	53
Whitewash	Grahame Davies	60
Notes and Acknowledgements		67

Preface

My grandmother Eva was a remarkable person although, when I was growing up, I didn't always appreciate having to listen to her repertoire of songs (she liked rousing hymns and sentimental ballads), stories about her childhood and snippets of scandal from the Sunday newspapers. Nor did I always welcome her 'wrap-around' embrace, particularly when my school-friends were nearby! I found her ability to remember long narrative poems very impressive, but rather embarrassing, especially when she insisted on performing them in a 'thrilling' and 'theatrical' voice, with accompanying dramatic gestures. I preferred it when she stuck to reciting shorter poems and it was one of these which she wrote out for me when I was trying to collect entries to fill a crisp new autograph book.

My passion for autographs vanished as quickly as it came, and the book lay hidden for many years, until I found it one day at the back of a cupboard, and stopped to read the long-forgotten rhymes and the careful, childish signatures. I had thought that my grandmother's verse was her own composition, but I now realised that this wasn't very likely. I found out later that it came from an American poet, Henry Van Dyke, popular when my grandmother was a little girl:

> There are many kinds of love, as many kinds of light,
> And every kind of love makes a glory in the night.
> There is love that stirs the heart, and love that gives it rest,
> But the love that leads life upward is the noblest and the best.

The words had obviously appealed to her, with their recognition that love takes many different forms. My grandmother was a survivor: she came through a bitter divorce and the horrors of two world wars, but nevertheless retained an irrepressible enthusiasm for romantic stories and films. She had good reason to understand love – and longing – in all their various aspects. The poems in this collection would certainly have spoken to her as they will to readers of a new generation with fresh concerns and preoccupations, but the same underlying emotions.

It is an anthology which ranges widely across love in all its guises, as each contributor brings a fresh and unique perspective to an age-old phenomenon. The joy and exuberance as well as the intensity and frustration of young love are beautifully summed up by Gwyneth Glyn, in a poem sequence which conveys the riskiness of commitment, and the bravado needed to cover the disappointment of unrequited love, a theme also taken up by Jenny Sullivan, who selects orange as the most appropriate colour for rejection. In quieter mood, Jenny's 'Between the Lines' brings out all the fragility of a romantic love threatened by the First World War, and it is a relief to learn that the young couple in the poem survived to become parents and grandparents. Daisy would have been their great-great-granddaughter and it is for Daisy that Jenny wrote '*Briallu'r Dydd*', a song to celebrate all that we hope for when a baby is born.

Christine Evans, too, focuses on the miracle of new life, but perhaps with a darker emphasis, reminding us in 'Taking Flowers' that loss is the other face of love. We don't know the details of Cara's loss in Christine's poem

'Separation'; we only know that life without her father is a painful reminder of past happiness, and a struggle to find new meaning.

For all its lyrical celebration of love (how many readers will have connected romance and maths?), Rex Harley's sequence is tinged with nostalgia and regret, the sense that it is possible to remember, but not recreate, the past: the people important to us when we are young; first aching love and the long golden summers of our childhood. They leave their mark but are ultimately beyond recovery.

That same feeling of regret haunts Julie Rainsbury's evocation of the old schoolhouse where she now lives, with its silent echo of children's games and voices from a bygone age. Julie identifies obsession as a form of love taken to extremes, and the 'magpie-dapper' subject of 'The Man Who Loved Birds' is the victim of a passion which destroys him.

Bird imagery – magpies, swans, curlews – pervades Owen Sheers's poems about adult relationships and attraction, and pain, whether physical or psychological, is never far away even in his most lyrical work.

It is love for a beautiful but defenceless creature which is the theme of Chris Kinsey's sequence of poems. The greyhound, subject to the whims of human fashion and cruelty, is every bit as fragile and precious as the teenage ego or the newborn baby.

For Susan Richardson, dissatisfaction with the quality of Welsh snow leads to a wild and dangerous flirtation with the whiteness and purity of Norway. Like many a youthful passion, an early blaze leads to a rapid cooling and a realisation that perfection is illusory. The snow which dazzled in its initial brilliance is surprisingly shallow, and quickly sullied by contact with real life. Susan's connection with Scotland is echoed, with new poignancy, in Grahame Davies's poem, 'Coronach', where he reminds us that language is as vulnerable as human love, and its passing no less tragic. The purity and single-mindedness of childhood is the subject of yearning for lost innocence in 'Whitewash' whilst 'Prayer', which brings *Poems of Love and Longing* to a close, is an expression of universal human aspiration.

And with that prayer, the wheel turns full circle. If perfect love is golden and warmed by the sun's rays, perhaps longing is silver, dazzling and iridescent by moonlight but subject too to night terrors. The interplay between night and day in Gillian Clarke's poem sequence, which opens the collection, is a reminder that love and longing are complementary and that, at their interface, there is a subtle blending which sometimes makes them hard to tell apart.

Viv Sayer
Editor, Pont Books

GILLIAN CLARKE

Room

A lamp
on a table
in a room
in a house
between hills
and the grey Atlantic
turning its pages.

A book open
under the lamp
on the table,
where the trees step in
to the room
in the house
on the hill.

Now dusk darkens
the pages
of the sea
till nothing's left
but a book
on a table
in a golden room.

Love at Livebait

That time she stepped out of the rain
into the restaurant,
beautiful in her black coat,
her scarf that shocking pink
of fuchsia, geranium, wild campion,
and he at the table,
his eyes her mirror.

She said she didn't know then –
but the light in her knew,
and the diners, the cutlery, the city,
the waiter filling the glasses with a soft
lloc-lloc and an updance of bubbles,
and the fish in their cradles of ice,
oceans in their eyes,

and all the colours of light
in a single diamond
slid down the window to merge with another.
Later they turned together
into the city and the rain.
On the pavement one fish scale winked,
bright enough to light half the planet.

Gravity

Still arguing whose fault it was
after all these years,
an old sweet war to return to
those times when it ought to be perfect.
Like tonight,

when the owl cries in the garden
and they think of her heart-face,
her bloody claws.
The moon looks in through wet glass
and dissolves in tears.

He says it was all down to poetry,
the cat-suit buttoned to knuckles, to throat.
She says he planned it,
fetching chairs from the empty house,
going back for a last look.

He drew the bolts on the back door
and led her into the night garden,
to check the sky for Orion,
the air for that malted brew
of bonfires and *Brains Dark*.

Looking up made them dizzy.
They leaned against gravity.
The planet turned a fraction
and they were done for,
falling, falling.

Barn

Sawdust spins in the sun-shaft,
on his hair, his shoulders, his busy hands,
gold-dust on his father's old boiler suit.

He and the electric plane, they can't hear her,
or see her wait, paddling in the angel-curls,
steam rising from her cupped hands.

He draws oiled steel through timber
over and over till it's smooth as skin,
and before silence, before it all stops, before hello,

yellow sings in the air like the gorse
that is never out of season,
small flames against the dark.

Wings

She wakes suddenly in the night
to feel the moon's glaciers
slide their silvers over the bed
engulfing the two of them,

and touches him to be sure, scared
at the silence between the phrasing
of a breath, his shoulder cold,
his moonlit hand marble.

The early hours. She listens, lifts her head
to lose the muffle of feathers,
the crack of interstellar static,
the knock of her own heart,

and his beating steadily over the tundra,
paired for life, migrating through the night
in falling feathers of snow, his shoulder blades
warm again, wingless, human.

JULIE RAINSBURY

Hardly a Haiku

I can't write a love
poem – but if I could then
it would be for you.

Heart to Heart

At the start, your heart-shaped
valentine, all hearts and flowers,
vowed, hand on heart,
you'd lost your heart to mine.
Sweetheart, you cooed,
little heartling, heartlet,
I've set my heart on you.
Cupid's dart has pierced
my heart. I'm heartsick,
adore you: from the bottom
of my heart, with all my heart,
heart and soul. I chart
your every breath. Be gentle-
hearted, have a heart,
my Queen of Hearts, set
this hungry heart to rest.
Heart-stopper.
You pluck my heartstrings,
make them sing. Be mine,
let our two hearts entwine
and never part. I love you,
cross my heart . . .

I learned each word by heart.
Your sugared Love Heart promises,
so heartfelt and heart-warming,
I took them all to heart.
You really played your part,

put all your heart into the art
of love, wore your heart
upon your sleeve. Open-hearted,
you were ... all heart.
Tall, dark and handsome too –
a fine, brave-hearted heart-throb.
I thought your heart in the right place.
My heartbeat quickened,
all a-flutter. Heart pounding,
I took heart and, heart in mouth,
followed my heart. I believed
you were THE ONE AND ONLY
ONE ... one after my own heart.
Soft-hearted, I should have
hardened my weak heart
into a wooden heart, a cold
heart of stone. Instead,
this heart of blood and flesh
became a heart of glass.
My heart's ease shattered
into heartache, sleepless nights
heart-searching, crying my heart out.
You Knave of Hearts! You heart failure!
In my heart of hearts, I think
I'd always heard the faint heart
murmur of your cheating heart.
Heavy-hearted, heart-sore, I've borne
your heart-rending heart attack.
Empty-hearted, I recall each word
spoken, each meaningless love token.
Now I find you heartless
and myself heartbroken.

Hen Ysgol

Sound again burbles, muted, from the yard
yet no-one passes by the road nor waits
to rap upon our door. Only rough-carved
initials tumble stone, Cilgerran slate,
these soft-gold window arches gouged and starred
by silent histories, small loves and hates.
A pheasant in the wood could not sustain
that cry, wind through trees conjure a refrain

like children's voices lilting high and low –
a sense, half-heard, of laughter, abrupt yells,
running footsteps and chants – the ebb and flow
of playtime spilled across Parc Bach. A bell's
toll echoes: an elusive undertow
through our new term of childless days. A well,
sealed way back, still whispers spells of water,
a register of long lost sons and daughters.

The Man Who Loved Birds

He was such a magpie-dapper man
until skeins of geese ensnared him.
Their plaintive passing made air rhythmic –
shivered silk. He tracked each arrow's fletch
sky-west beyond the sunset. Always one for sorrow,
solitary, a blood-rush beat caught his measured breath.
He teetered on high boulders, arms wide-spread,
giddied by ideas way above his station.

Neck stretched to upland cloud, he grew aware
of others: flocks of pterodactyl, archangel,
revealed by his binoculars. He became attuned.
At dawn, at dusk, he listened eagerly to voices
from the distance: four or five piped notes, a code
carried over scree, along the cwm. Haunting. Secret.
He admired such regularity, those rituals of song.
Sometimes he laughed aloud, a murmuration to rival
thrushes in the heather. He tried to behave, recorded
tamer sightings in a notebook: buzzard, wren and raven,
occasional wheatears, meadow pipits. His head fogged
with ornithology, stuffed full of pluckings, downy as a duvet.

Each day he stirred seed, berries, nuts in melted lard,
fashioned patties to hang in his garden. He tempted
sparrow, robin, finch, wagtail, pigeon, blackbird, watched
a murder of tattered crows scrap high above the sycamore.
The shadow wings flapped closer, their flicker-fluttering
confused him. The kitchen became slick with fat. He sucked
his fingers, picked crumbs. Blue tits peered at him, pecked
putty from his window-frames. Swifts slammed into nests
that clung tight beneath his eaves. Escape was impossible.

He quilled a bird-print charm across his greasy surfaces,
studied its ogham, trilled rhapsodies of bird-name
like a lover: *my dove, whitethroat, my waxwing*.

He struggled to stay grounded but often couldn't help himself.
Arms raised, with tilted thumbs, swallow-tailed feet turned
outward, he'd swoop thermals in the wind-tunnel by Asda.
Air thrummed. *Bird brain!* children called as he hopped,
bold, along the kerbstones. Earthbound, he itched,
obsessively checked his skin for signs of plumage.

His dreams caged exotica from reference books in the library.
These were so much bigger, brighter, increasingly awkward
to control: flamingo, albatross, parakeet, condor –
all had minds of their own. He tried to set them free,
traced their images on sheets of Izal, let them glide
across the fence to gather in next-door's yard.

There were complaints but he was beyond now,
kite-high with anticipation. He screeched,
hooted through the tarnished beak of his letter box,
cawed and clawed at knock-down-ginger boys
who stole his gold top. Eyes followed him everywhere,
spied on him – beady black, white amber.

At last, perched on the window ledge, his bones
shuffled their anatomy. He felt his spine click, an ache
of fusing vertebrae. His skull rang, fragile as an eggshell.
He preened, ruffled new prismatic scales, out-stared
the sun's brass iris. Ecstatic, he warbled like a nightingale,
fluted incantations of flight, confident as winter's mistle-thrush.
Each note was clear, sustained. When he heard their coming
on a host of drumming wings, he spiralled out to join them

. . . unleashed in a madrigal of light . . .

Show

I

The models walk,
high-heeled as curlews
stalking a narrow shore.

We watch, spectators
at a slow-motion tennis match
as they turn,

flex the featherless wings
of their shoulders
and slip between the curtains,

leaving the crocodile pit of cameras
flashing their teeth for more.

II

I leave you sitting to the mirror
like a pianist to the piano,
lifting the mascara brush
to paint your lashes from fine to bold.

Pulling the door on this scene
I walk down the corridor
to wait in the bar for you to join me.
And when you do, it happens once more;

The fall of the dress, the jewellery,
early stars against the dusk of your skin,
all of it leaves me surrendered,
if just for a second, as you walk in,

to the spell, the artful hocus-pocus,
and to you standing there
one shoulder bare,
setting the room about you out of focus.

Winter Swans

The clouds had given their all –
two days of rain and then a break
in which we walked,

the waterlogged earth
gulping for breath at our feet
as we skirted the lake, silent and apart,

until the swans came and stopped us
with a show of tipping in unison.
As if rolling weights down their bodies to their heads

they halved themselves in the dark water,
icebergs of white feather, paused before returning again
like boats righting in rough weather.

'They mate for life' you said as they left,
porcelain over the stilling water. I didn't reply
but as we moved on through the afternoon light,

slow-stepping in the lake's shingle and sand,
I noticed our hands, that had, somehow,
swum the distance between us

and folded, one over the other,
like a pair of wings settling after flight.

The Rest

You lay your head in the hollow
between my chest and open shoulder,
the right and yet the wrong one too;
the one that came apart
years before you knew of me, or I of you.

The one that aches in the rain,
that stops my hand from reaching my spine.
the one that's healed but can't forget
the echoes of that pain.

But here, you say, is where you can rest,
and I have to agree that this
is where you fit the best;
within those places I've come apart,
within the woundings of my past.

Song

If we were magpies, love,
and some day a bright bait caught your eye
and you were taken in a magpie trap,

a siren in a cage, then I would stay,
perch above you, spread my wings in the rain
and fan you with my feathers in the sun.

And when the others came,
drawn by the oil spill of your plumage,
the darkness of your eye,

I'd watch them strut in,
squawking to their doom
to find themselves trapped.

All night I'd listen to their confusion,
the beat of wing on wire, until the morning
and the farmer came to wring their lives away.

And through the winter I would feed you,
dropping the mites like kisses to your beak.
And in the spring I'd sing, touch my wings to yours

while we waited for that day
when the farmer, realising at last as all men must
that love is all there is to save,

will open the door to your cage
and let you walk out to me,
where I will be waiting
to help you try your wings again.

CHRIS KINSEY

HOUNDLOVE

Foresight

I fell in love with the dog
on the pub sign.
Forty years later
she bounded out of make-believe.

Getting to Know the Greyhound

The slightest sniff makes your muscles ripple.
Squirrels set you arrow-alert
then you soften, move like quicksand.

A kingfisher flies low, close to the bank.
Overtaking its reflection, it falters
on a spillage of turquoise.

The turquoise walks off the water
flutters into a wrap-around skirt.
A wolf-whistle shrills afternoon silent.

'What a beaut!'
You reel back, hide from the man
with noughts and crosses on his neck.

'Ex-racer? – Winner?'
'Don't know her history,
only had her a fortnight.'

'Bet she's a good rabbiter.'
Coaxing you from behind my legs,
we walk on. He calls,

'Can I have pups off of her?'
Nodding at the pram I say,
'You'll have to stick to babies.'

The woman grins, but he frowns.
'She's been spayed,' I say.
'Shame – if I had a pup

I wouldn't do nothing cruel –
just a bit of lamping.
Gotta feed these two!'

Loosed for the first time, you rip
through ripe grasses, stand paw-crooked,
as rabbits white-tail into hard earth.

I open my arms and call with all my lungs.
You're instantly in my shadow's pool,
pressing like a strong current, lapping my fingers.

Race Developed

(For U.A. Fanthorpe)

My red pedal car wasn't fast enough
so I stripped my pram to freewheels and chassis,
steered the wind with washing line,
drove a racing car round the doctor's feet –
full Grand Prix – whilst he listened to Gran's chest.
He told me of Stirling Moss,
Sundays spent rallying minis.
The year Foinavon won the Grand National
I was going to be a jockey,
a stud farm on the lounge floor
and only Arkle away from a complete
card set of steeplechase champions.
Then it was bikes: two-strokes, four-strokes,
a 125, a 250 RD and the showroom's
Ducati I never had off centre stand –
too short of leg and cash.
Now I free two tall greyhounds:
they fix sights, power down,
accelerate faster than a Ferrari.
Wind-sleeked, nerve-wired,
genetically tweaked for speed and yaw,
they come back at an easy lope
ready to be fireside thoroughbreds.

Prompts

(in memory of 'Jaydee', our first greyhound)

Now you race with the cloud shadows.
You're in the spring-back of trodden grass,
the snuffle of wind through the thicket,
the pricked ears of flowering gorse,
the crooks of rising fern
and the bronze flanks of hill bracken.
You're in forest mists, mosses' cool siphoning of stars,
wind's attempts to finger-print a lake,
the brush of blown willow-down
and the tease of forget-me-nots.

Elemental

Two shadows cast from Swansea racetrack.
Not twins; different elements –

'Tango' is silica, obsidian,
natural glass,
a quick-cooled volcano,
high-gloss, scalpel sharp,
softened in the mould of much stroking.

'Woody' is all the tropes of carbon,
from smouldering peat
to rare, black diamond,
fluid as oil, soft as charcoal,
your lines merge and smudge with mine.

Sleeping with the Beast

(for 'Woody', who slipped through many homes before choosing us)

'Be so kind as to bring me a rose, for none grows hereabouts.'
('Beauty' in the traditional tale.)

It all started with eating wild blueberries –
My door isn't often open.
Sometimes invisible hands draw it back …

A scratch of claws on floorboards,
A snort at the foot of the bed and you bound alongside,
nuzzle my hands, nudge me to uncurl.

Tonight you put your muzzle to my throat,
press your glossy head under my chin
then stretch a paw, pin my chest.

I smooth matted fur, stroke tender spots,
start undoing the curse which makes you cower.
Your breathing's ragged but regular –

a whiff of bone on your lips.
Strong claws scrabble air,
rapid eye movements flutter my neck,

you roll over, offer me your throat
and the two white roses
which crown your chest.

Recipe for a Greyhound

Don't think – you won't be quick enough.

Settle,
    sink –
hounds spring from the deepest sleep.

Make your mind a boundless park.
Pay attention to trees, thickets
and rising grass – undulations are irresistible.

Let the sun set, leave it grow wild,
the spring needs time to pool.
Get used to the dark.

When you can see moonlight
fashion the finest bones
from the best calcium,

tie the ligaments, tune the muscles,
conjure the sprung spine,
charge it with a lightning spark,

give it a heart that can hold thunder
and stroke it into grace.
Leave it lie.

Go back to the park,
wait for the first leaf to spin like a prayer wheel,
whistle softly, your dog will come whiffling.

Offer your hand, your scent.

Hindsight

Interlaced like Celtic design
the hounds and I run dreams
to reality and slip the leash
of time.

REX HARLEY

LOVE

I

I am seven
and I know
what love is.

It is a red tray
made of tin and
patched with little
yellow flowers.

Soon she will tap
at the bedroom door,
come in, and place it
gently where I sit
waiting.

She will smile and speak words, but
all I will hear is
the way she says them
because

her voice is delicious
as the custard in the bowl on the tray in her hands and
   the custard

is made with milk from a bottle with a gold top and in the
    bottle
is cream so thick it will not pour so you dip your finger in and
eat it straight
and —
wait!

She's here.

I am seven
and I know love.
Its name is . . .

II

Beatrice. I found a photograph
behind a barricade of yellowed
letters in my mother's desk.
Taller than I recalled: no wonder
I looked up to her. But was she
beautiful? Was she the girl
who fashioned my desires?

I took a magnifying glass
and held it to her grainy face.
The features vanished in
a blizzard; a black and white
kaleidoscope. Memory itself
disintegrates; but still I hear
that voice, unwavering.

III

Maths defeated me.
It had rules.
There was no room
for manoeuvre.

You could never talk
your way out
of a problem.
It was right or

it was not. The one
and only thing
I finally got
to grips with was

simultaneous
equations.
I was the same with girls. Useless.

Until one summer
holiday
and Sarah who
came from Fulham.

She had a way with
words. 'Wouldn't
you like to know?'
she'd taunt me and my

knees turned to water.
It took me

ages to slip
my arm round her:

fear of breaking rules.
She didn't mind
waiting, and was glad to teach me

simultaneous
equations:
>   Thought (mine)   + lips (hers)   = kiss
>   Action (hers)   + lips (mine)   = bliss
>   Solution = 'Wouldn't *you* like to know?'

I'd just mastered this
maths of love
when she packed off
back to Fulham.

For a while we wrote
chaste letters
in our neatest
handwriting and

I lamented my
so slow learning.
Girls and maths
were hard again

and I was left to
dream the things
I *could* have learned
had time allowed.

IV

I fell under the spell of silent films;
could walk like Charlie Chaplin; bought a pair
of glasses just like Harold Lloyd's; but what
I loved was Buster Keaton's dead-pan stare.
I gazed unblinking at my mirror-face;
no hint of feeling flickered in my eyes.
And so, by hiding everything I felt,
I learned to be a master of disguise.

It was a phase, of course. But even when
the clothes were shed, the worn-out image thrown,
I could not lose the skill that I'd acquired:
the art of being one, and all alone.

V

The little ferry is layered
paint on paint. Scuffs and
cracks reveal the colours
of summers past.

Hidden deep, close to the bare
wood, is my childhood: spray
from the bow, a hand trailed
in the water.

Every summer it crests
the currents and the wash
of bigger boats, shore to
estuary shore,

and I climb aboard,
let it carry me out
to a stretch of still water
where the land vanishes.

If I could see my own
face, it would have skin
as smooth and untroubled
as the cloudless sky;

and love and hope would
keep company; and she
would be waiting for me
on the other side.

GWYNETH GLYN

In love (NOT)

I'm not in love, you know, I'm really not.
OK, you cross my mind sometimes, so what?
Your smile does kind of make my face feel hot ...
I'm not in love, you know, I'm really not.

I'm not in love, you know, come on, get real!
I dream about you sometimes – so? Big deal!
I might have scratched your name into my heel ...
I'm not in love, you know, come on, get real!

I'm not obsessed, you know, I'm not obsessed.
So what if it's your eyes I like the best?
And who cares if you're fitter than the rest?
I'm not obsessed, you know, I'm not obsessed.

I fancy you. That's all. A little bit.
'Cause when we talk, my clothes don't seem to fit,
and everything I say comes out like shit.
I fancy you. That's all. A little bit.

I'm not in love, you know, I'm not in love.
It isn't always you I'm thinking of.
Though I did nick your stupid bobbly glove ...
I'm not in love, you know.

Am I?
Love?

If I were . . .

If I were the wind,
honest as the wind,
I'd follow you,
swallow you,
all of you in,
if I were the wind.

If I were the sun,
brazen as the sun,
I'd heat you up,
eat you up,
beat you like a drum,
If I were the sun.

Lips like a lullaby,
don't want to rush you.
Bit like a butterfly,
don't want to crush you.

If I were the rain,
relentless as the rain,
I'd soak you
and cloak you,
like smoke on your skin,
if I were the rain.

If I were just myself,
simple as myself,
would you hold me,
plain old me,
and silver-and-gold me,
or fold me
and mould me
into somebody else?
If I were just myself?

Belong

Behind my heart,
beneath my soul,
between my selves,
a void so small,
yet infinite
as the Black Hole.

It has no name,
it swallows sound,
it screams its silence
in the dark.
It changes shape,
it knows no-one,
longs to be known
by none.

Yet if I dare
to stare
too long
into the bleak
I find
that which I seek;
a glimmering,
glowing,
growing
glare.

I belong there;
between my selves,
behind my heart,
beneath my soul,
where Something,
Someone,
who's more myself
than I,
remains,
to sing my name
into the sky.

Red and Blue

I'm supposed to be writing a poem,
scribbling something in blue.
But the ink runs red
from my heart to my head,
and instead I just write
'Me 4 U'.

I'm supposed to be writing a poem,
with metaphors, rhythm and rhyme.
But my mind is a muddle,
and I just want a cuddle,
and nothing much sounds like your name.

My poem is yet to be started;
I see yours is already done.
And I'll know from the start
it's not me in your heart
but that fart-bag in class B1.

JENNY SULLIVAN

Rejection

Rejection is orange
Not, as one might think,
Grey and nondescript.
It is the vivid orange of
A council workman's jacket.
A coat of shame that says
'he doesn't want you'.

Rejection tastes like ashes
Acrid, bitter.
It sounds
Like the whisper of voices
Behind my back.
'He didn't want her.
He dumped her.'

It feels
Like the scraping of fingernails
On a blackboard,
Not ache or stab of pain
But like having
a layer of skin missing.

Rejection looks like – me,
I suppose.
Slightly leftover
Like the last, curled crust
Of cucumber sandwich
When all the guests
Have gone.

Unrequited

If love is good and kisses free
Why is it you don't fancy me?
Love is painful, unrequited,
My life is permanently blighted.

I worship you from much too far,
I watch you drive past in your car.
I love you with my soul and heart.
Tell me, why are we apart?

The way your hair curls at the back,
Oh, what assets do I lack?
If only you could spare a glance
My heart would positively dance.

Perhaps it's just you haven't seen
(my hair is red and eyes are green).
Why is it you completely miss me
When all I want is you to kiss me?

Oh, unimaginable dreams!
I'm separating at the seams.
Smacking my head against a wall,
You haven't noticed me at all.

I've followed you today to try
To nonchalantly catch your eye,
Toss a blithe and cheery greeting –
But heavens – who is this you're meeting?

I don't believe what I can see!
The truth, they say, will set me free.
Can't get my breath – I'm fit to choke –
You're holding hands with another bloke!

War Cemetery, Herouville

Wooden gate
worn soft as flannel to the touch.
Curved path. This gentle,
hidden way, this green-ness,
did not prepare us.
This was, they said, a small one.
Birdsong and breath dwindled.
In pin-drop hush we read:
'Beloved', 'Known Only Unto God', 'Much Loved'.
Mistake.
How could we stop?
Which, pass by?
We paced a thousand cancelled childhoods,
a thousand unborn sons.
Sacrificial stones,
and at their heart
a crimson flower bled.
Trees sighed.
The dying sun coaxed shadows
to fall in dusk's communion.
We loved them, strangers all,
and left them to their
hard-won peace.

Between the Lines

When she died, in her crowded, empty house,
we found, in battered albums, postcards
spanning two lives, a war, and love.
Amid a life's detritus, I sat enthralled
at glimpses of their unknown lives.
'Dear Eva'. Oh, such guarded lines
penned by 'Your friend Harold';
but later, closer, 'Harry'. Then,
six months on, there's boldness!
Love revealed by two diffident,
lightly pencilled kisses.
Eva first, then 'Eve': in Harry's neat
meticulous hand, the cards became
familiar, daring, almost – 'with love,
Your Harry'.

1914: he enlisted (of course),
posed in shapeless khaki,
regiment as yet unknown,
gazing nobly up, up-stage-left, peaked cap
shading a too-young face,
ready to Do His Duty.
He did.
Sent gauzy organza cards from hell
– 'Dear Eve, Your loving Harry'.
A hand-embroidered
tulle confection – '*Gloire Aux Allies*';
sepia women home-firelit, reading
letters from the Front, a ghostly Tommy
floating in the margins.

Sentimental verse imposed on feeling.

Few words from Harry, but all full-charged,
still in his neat and careful hand.

Gassed: his own lungs drowning him. But
still, the silver lining – a Blighty pass,
for convalescence and a wedding: Eve and her Harry,
their future mortgaged to gas, shells,
mud and misery. Hope and knowledge
dauntless in their eyes.

They sent him back, of course,
two months on. Warm bodies essential nourishment
for cold and mud, blood, death, shrapnel
and futility: a few yards gained or lost.
But first, a card from Kinmel Camp, April 1916.
Easing transition to hell, perhaps.
A simple message home
requesting his light boots, that's all.
Perhaps his feet hurt.
'Please try and send them, dear,' across the top.
'It don't matter if they need mending, they will do them here.'
'Love Harry' and three kisses.

Truth shows in sprawling scrawl: untidy, scored-out,
words misspelled; the postcard stained and blotted.

Between the lines:
'Eve, I love you, miss you, need you.
Eve, I am desolate without you.'
Light boots.
'Please try and send them, dear.'

Cân Briallu'r Dydd – Daisy's Song

You are the sum of our past and our present,
The flower of the future is yours to command.
Sunshine and moonlight are simply your birthright
And a necklace of stars to keep in your hand.

You we shall nurture, we'll help you to blossom;
To be all that you can be – and help you to grow;
Help you to learn, to be proud and be forthright,
And love you enough to – in time – let you go.

You are our hope, our new leaf, young and tender,
You are the flower we're given to hold;
You are our gift from the past to the future;
You'll be the joy in our hearts when we're old.

Daisy, *Briallu*, our past and our present,
Daisy, our flower, we are yours to command.
Sunshine and laughter are simply your birthright –
And a necklace of stars to keep in your hand.

CHRISTINE EVANS

Angharad's First Spring

Light loves her skin:
sticks to it like leaf-fur.

She is trying now to catch words
at the mouth, as they soar and bubble,
to trap and play with them in fingers
whose own magic she is still exploring.

She laughs aloud. White buds
are breaking through her gums.

I put her back in your arms.

Asking the Bees

(For Emma Bee)

Last fuchsias at the back of Cristin
Full of a steady, unseen, growing hum

That lulls the woman on the bench
Almost to a summer drowse.

She shuts her eyes on sea-glitter
On all the patterns she translates into paint,

One hand resting on her belly
As if fingertips could feel through flesh

The dance of cells, could recognise
What tiny unique self's unfolding there.

She wonders, *what will the gales of autumn
Bring? Where might winter's tides beach us?*

*Is this the path I should have followed?
After this baby, how will the world be changed?*

But the bees' prophecies are all
Of discoveries and the taste

Of colours; flowers' heavinesses,
The ardent gold of pollen;

Of summer safely gathered in and stored,
Of ripening, and glut, and brim.

Of new directions, rightness, honey.

Taking Flowers

Nid i'w Anghofio on the gate, and a grave
like the roof of a small dolls' house
for the infant brothers of Rhosgoch:
Owen, one year; Lewis, three months;
Gwilym and Bedwyr, aged three, and two months;
Danial, twenty-two days.

In the old part, heavy quiet and crosses
padded with lichen, last narrow beds
plumped with pillows of soft growth,
screens of nettles, bracken, bramble.
Mould age-spots grand slate boxes.
Evan Evans' stone is cracked across.

Our way back is between hedges
where beech leaves curl like bats
waiting for night. A stone lane lined with ivy
demurely holding out stiff posies
of poisonous black fruit
above bare roots that clasp, and cling, and hold.

Miss Burder

She died the day that long hot
summer broke. It was expected;
looked-for perhaps in suffocating nights
and aching August afternoons
when even here, far west, we thought we heard
all tender greenness shrivelling.

Each week since I've walked to where
she watched the sun slide down
to douse itself in cool salt water.
Those endless miles of living ocean;
and then the first stars, always bravest
on the far rim of the dark.

Now the sea is pewter, hammered smooth
by the rain-heavy sky, and wind
moans round blank walls. The door
no longer opens on her laughter
and the warmth of her clear eyes.

The light in the lap of Anelog
is out. The road to Bodisaf
becomes a dead end.

Separation

Cara on the beach alone
has watched the slow tide creep
and lick her feet, and crawl
away again to sleep.
Since the others ran off, jeering,
trampling the sand-garden she'd made
she has crouched in a cave
scooped to the shape of the wind,
staring at colours in trickles of sand.

On her wet hand, it was a soft grey glove
but studied closer, light picks out
crystal, pink, brown eggshell specks,
a darker and a paler blue.
There are glinting triangles of green glass
and shells like tiny babies' fingernails
or flaked almonds, with their pearly shine.

And all at once, she is whisked back
to a kitchen safe against the storm of winter,
helping with the Christmas cake. Her fingers
lift and sift the sand like fine warm flour.
She shakes the memory away. No.
Anyway, it's more like soil, the sort
you buy in bags, for planting bulbs.
'A spring surprise,' he'd said, and how
their secret present would be growing in the dark
all through the months until Mum's birthday.

The February Gold came true, but by then
it was too late for anyone to notice.
She flings the sand in a wild scatter,
picks up a driftwood root clenched to a fist
so when further on she finds an old egg
where a grey thing's stilled in its squirming,
(naked head and limbs, its eyes still sealed
as if with plastic), her arm
lifts like a puppet's, smashes down.

She hates this place, the shrieking birds,
the seals that spy on her with goggly eyes
and snort like cross old teachers, make her jump.
Not knowing why or where her father's gone,
grit in her eyes, she stumbles back to where
last year was fun, and jokes at breakfast.

But months later, underneath her pillow
her mother feels and draws into the light
a palm-sized oval of clear glass.
A keepsake of the beach, their holiday,
she thinks, but then feels how
it could be held against the heat of nightmare;
its shape enduring in the broken dark

as if the sea could weep, and seal its tears
into a shape as strong as stone
to leave on an island shore, move on.

SUSAN RICHARDSON

TRUE NORTH

I

Unrequited – Cwmbran, South Wales

Winter's stood me up again –
I was sold a pack of lies.
I've got a hanky of snow, not a blanket
and some underachieving ice.

I've got a miserable sniffle of winter –
a sneeze of flakes and rows
of icicles already dripping
like a runny nose.

I want a mature winter
that won't beat a hasty retreat,
that commits to the months from November to March,
that won't get cold feet.

I want a winter to make me tingle
and quiver and feel enchanted.
I want a lake and I want to take
the thickness of its ice for granted.

I want a real snowman
who'll stick around for a bit,
not one whose muscles turn to slush
at the merest hint of grit.

If winter here keeps spurning me,
I'm going to seek, henceforth,
the snowman of my dreams in a land of extremes:
I'm heading North.

II

First Flush: Å, The Lofoten Islands, Norway

Midnight –
and the sky's still bright as daylight.
This is no half-hearted half-light,
no grimy grey frayed-at-the-edges
overwashed underwear light.
This is no lacklustre dusk:
this is up-front, in-your-face light,
a high-latitude-with-attitude light.

I'm flushed with light,
lush with light,
hushed speechless with light.
I throw open the shutters of my lungs
and gulp this light which sizzles
on the tundra of my tongue
'til I hum with light,
pulse with light –
it lifts me like vitamins.

I zing in this bling of light.
My hair is a tinsel string of light,
my tonsils tingle with light –
I suck on the Strepsil of the sun,
then gorge six more courses of light
plus a froth-topped shot of light
that will keep me awake for at least eight nights.
I'm sleeplessness on stilts –
like the fishing hut where I stay, I teeter
and tilt with light.

I'm a whale of light
flipping my forked orca tail of light,
exhaling light from my blowhole.
I'm an auk of light,
      soaring,
supported on a cushion of light that transforms
into a slide down which I glide
into a roaring northern sea of light.

I'm a giant stockfish rack of light.
I've hit the arctic jackpot of light.
I am Å –
an exclamation of light,
a madly, deeply, in-light-with-light
        sigh.

III

Lovers' Tiff: the Isle of Skye, Scotland

Clouds swoop, snatch
the crags and peaks, claw
at the gabbro, gobble
the humps of the Hebrides.
Sixty billion midges breed and feed
on the drenched horned heads of cattle.
Gannets dive
to a depth of five hundred feet.
Waterfalls course down
Kilt Rock's pleats.

Seals, otters,
deer, sheep
go two-by-two into the ferry at Uig.
Drops the size of rocks wake
the ghosts of the Norse invaders. They leap
aboard the corpse of their longboat
and promise to stop marauding
if they make it back to Norway.

The Old Man of Storr's soaked to his stony neck.
In Flodigarry, Flora's bones are forced
to the surface, then hurled
four thousand miles
over the sea from Skye.

The Blue Men of the Minch conjured this.
They squelched
from their underwater caves,
wrecked six ships and now stretch
their scaly arms
           towards me.
They'll drag
   me under –
unless I can divert them
with this porous verse,
this spongy rhyme.

IV

Casting a Spell: Snaefellsnes Peninsula, Iceland

Five months now I've known you,
yet you still cause my heart to drum
like the feathers of a courting snipe,

with your silver streams –
giant snails' trails that creep
down the sides of your mountains.

With your black sand beach
and its seaweed streaked with pink,
like strands in a girl singer's hair.

With the lava plaits cascading
from the wise white head
of your sleeping glacier-volcano.

From you, I've learnt
that willows don't need to weep,
that a tree can be three inches tall.

I've learnt to be just as enthralled by lichen
as by basalt boulders like enormous peppercorns.
I've learnt to hear the grey moss breathe

as it feels itself turn green in the rain
and the murmur of ferns unfurling
in your cradle of craters.

I drink yarrow juice and wild thyme tea
and instantly see your *huldufólk* –
the elves which dwell with the gulls

on your cliffs' panpipe pillars.
I see bearded Bardur
who heeded the dwarf-talk in your caves,

gave up this mortal world and became
the guardian of your glacier.
And I see an old woman

who shakes the leather pouch tied to her waist,
then reads the meaning
in the sheep's bones it contains.

'Will the magic last?' I ask.
'When we're apart,
will our relationship still be a success?'

Like the lupins seeded in your eroded soil,
joy speeds through me
when she announces 'Yes'.

V

Every Time We Say Goodbye: Saariselkä, Finland

Firs that once were firm
now seem bored with the settled snow: they shrug
it off each branch to leave it,
forlorn, at their feet below.

Skis that, on the flat,
glide serenely side by side, now clash
when they reach a slope,
provoking a fatal downhill slide,

while pristine fields of snow get ruined
by canine urine stains. Blades
of grass poke through too, like sleep
pierced by pain.

And fell water falling free
is suddenly frozen, aborted
in mid-flow like words of remorse
which ought to be spoken.

I take my North home under a glass dome –
but it's filled with fake snow
and everyone's started to shake it.

GRAHAME DAVIES

Whitewash

When I was maybe seven or eight years old,
I undertook to do a job for Nain
and paint the small backyard which used to hold
the bins, the coal shed and the washing line.
Although Nain's house has long been cleared away,
the grimy stones on next door's wall still show
the square of whitewash once as clean as day,
my handiwork from three decades ago.
And every time I walk up Tabor Hill,
I have to touch the patch of tarnished paint
to get a speck of proof that I am still
connected to a time that had no taint;
because for me there's nothing now at all
as pure as childhood's whitewash on the wall.

Revisiting

It's twenty years exactly since I last
walked down these college corridors to class;
now, on a weekend visit to my past,
the lobby's new, the polished floor like glass.

And quiet too. But no surprise in that;
only the keenest would be here today
in study cubicles where I once sat,
a rainy Saturday in early May.

Businesslike, clean; no posters on the door,
no student scruffiness, except a trail
along the whole length of the gleaming floor:
the muddy footprints of a barefoot girl.

Along the passageway where I once went
to lectures, she came splashing from the street.
What panic, pain or pleasure could have sent
her through the mud with nothing on her feet?

But at the far end of the passageway,
a girl's belongings in a hasty pile –
a sign: 'Hamlet auditions here today' –
her overcoat, her unlaced boots, her file.

The marks our lives make never really go.
The tracks she left behind as she passed through
the corridor I walked, decades ago,
are transient as mine were, and as true.

Nothing is lost. I close the door, walk on.
She came, unshod, through dirty city rain,
to show the present and the past are one,
long-drowned Ophelia, alive again.

Coronach

The little breeze that whispers at the door
is saying that our language won't endure.
No locks or walls or fences now remain
to give her shelter in her old domain.

Should I be glad I lived to know this tongue
when she was beautiful, when she was young?
Or should I curse that I was born so late
that I must watch her dying, desolate?

❤

The gentle breeze that brings dry leaves to earth,
is saying death must follow every birth,
sooner or later, every thing must end;
all that you love is transient, my friend.

The breeze brings costly comfort in its song;
it says we should be glad it lived so long:
each language has a limit to its span;
you still can speak it, love it while you can.

❤

The breeze outside my window's brittle glass
says it's our fate to see this come to pass:
the final generation who will know
the living language – and who'll watch her go.

The breeze that stayed with us through thick and thin,
as cool as summer cotton on the skin,
has no more comfort in its quiet voice.
It's going to happen. You don't have a choice.

♥

The breeze brings heather fragrance from the hill
to mark the day the ancient words fall still,
it brings the tears of nature in its song
for one who kept it company so long.

It brings, in kindness, mist of shining grey,
to shroud our last indignity away.
It brings the gentlest rain that ever fell
the day the language whispers its farewell.

♥

The little breeze complains beneath the door
the words it loved aren't spoken any more.
At every lock it listens for their sound,
but they've been cleared away and can't be found.

It searches every corner, every place,
to find the words forgotten without trace,
and whispers to the heather in despair,
how beautiful, how beautiful they were.

Revelation

The winter's killed the foliage in the park,
and vistas open up that were not there
in summertime. And now the year's grown dark,
the leafless landscape of the world's laid bare.
The city's conscience that its growth concealed
lies plain to view like trash beneath the thorn:
discarded needles, cigarettes, revealed
with empty lager tins and last year's porn.
Let my discreet disguises die away
like woods in winter, leaving only trash,
laid clear and open to the light of day,
to be collected up and burned to ash.
And let the springtime find my soul next year
as cold as woods in winter, and as clear.

Prayer

Spirit, use me today,
not in some miracle
that would make others marvel
and would make me proud.

Not in the word of wisdom
that would stay in the mind
and make me always remembered.

Not in the heroic act
that would change the world for the better
and me for the worse.

But in the mundane miracles
of honesty and truth
that keep the sky from falling.

In the unremembered quiet words
that keep a soul on the path.

And in the unnoticed acts
that keep the world moving
slowly closer to the light.

Notes and Acknowledgements

The publishers gratefully acknowledge the co-operation and permission of the following:

Seren Books (for poems by Owen Sheers).

Page 2 'Livebait' is the name of a restaurant.

Page 4 'When the gorse is out of blossom, kissing is out of season.' (Old saying)

Page 9 The Welsh title 'Hen Ysgol' means 'Old School'.

Page 12 'Show' first appeared in *Skirrid Hill* (Seren, 2005)

Page 14 'Winter Swans' first appeared in *Skirrid Hill* (Seren, 2005)

Page 16 'Song' first appeared in *Skirrid Hill* (Seren, 2005)

Page 17 Chris Kinsey has made a two-minute digital story with the BBC about her greyhounds: http://www.bbc.co.uk/wales/audiovideo/

Page 20 Stirling Moss raced cars from 1948–1962.

The racehorse Foinavon won The Grand National in 1967 against odds of a hundred to one.

The racehorse Arkle is known as 'the greatest steeplechaser of all time'. He was compared to a greyhound for his 'style, athleticism and mobility'. When he was injured in 1966 he received thousands of cards and carrots.

Page 43 Harry survived the war, and he and Eva had two children. Their son, Robert, died at the age of seven; their daughter kept the postcards on which the poem is based. She was the mother of a second Robert, Jenny

Sullivan's husband. Harry and Eva died within two weeks of each other in 1960.

Page 45 *Briallu'r Dydd*, Daisy's Song. *Briallu'r Dydd* is an alternative Welsh name for the daisy, more usually known as *llygad y dydd*. Jenny Sullivan wrote this poem for her granddaughter Daisy, who was born on 15 July 2006.

Page 47 Emma helps her husband Steve run the Bird Observatory on Bardsey, and the unborn baby in this poem is their son Connor who is now five. Information about the island and its rich birdlife can be found at www.bbfo.org.uk

Page 49 The Welsh 'Nid i'w Anghofio' means 'Not to be Forgotten'.

Page 50 Miss Burder lived alone in a remote farmhouse owned by a London family for whom she had worked as a nanny for over forty years. Christine remembers her fondly: 'She missed children's company so I used to walk over the fields with my young son for tea, and we would play with her collection of Beatrix Potter figurines. I never called her by her first name.'

Page 51 This poem is set on Bardsey island where many families come on holiday in the summer. 'February Gold' is a miniature daffodil.

Page 56 Highland heroine Flora Macdonald famously helped 'Bonnie' Prince Charlie to escape from the Isle of Uist to Skye.

The Old Man of Storr is a strangely-shaped rock pinnacle on the Isle of Skye.

Page 57 According to legend, the Blue Men of the Minch are supernatural beings living in the stretch of water known as the Minch between the Inner and Outer Hebrides and mainland Scotland. They are believed to be responsible for sudden storms and shipwrecks.

Page 58 Many Icelanders believe in the existence of creatures known as *huldufólk* or hidden people.

Page 60 'Whitewash' is a translation of a poem from *Achos* (Barddas, 2005). 'Nain' (pronounced 'nine') is the north Walian word for 'grandmother'. Tabor Hill is situated in Coedpoeth, the village near Wrexham where the poet was born.

Page 63 'Coronach' is a partial translation of a poem in *Achos* (Barddas, 2005). '*Coronach*' is a Gaelic word which refers to the lamentation or dirge for the dead which accompanied funerals in the Highlands of Scotland and in Ireland. Here it is used as a lament for all endangered languages.

Page 65 'Revelation' is a translation of a poem from *Achos* (Barddas, 2005).

Page 66 'Prayer' is a translation of a poem from *Achos* (Barddas, 2005)